Walk through the Bible with Moses

Leena Lane and Chris Saunderson

walk through the sea with Moses

AN ACTION RHYME BOOK

Count! Count!
Count your sheep and your goats.
Bring your silver and gold, says Moses!

Count things in a line

Point to the sky

Look! Look!
A pillar of cloud.
Follow the cloud, with Moses.

March! March!
We're nearly there.
We've reached the Red Sea, with Moses.

Swing arms, lift up knees

Run! Run!
Let's cross the Red Sea!
We're crossing the sea, with Moses!

Draw circles in the air

Clip clop, clip clop!
The horses are coming.
The chariots are chasing Moses!

Splash! Splash!
The water is flowing.
The king's men cannot catch Moses.

Sweep arms upwards

Published in the UK by Scripture Union
207-209 Queensway, Bletchley, Milton Keynes, Bucks, MK2 2EB
ISBN 978 1 84427 254 9

First edition 2007

Copyright © 2007 Anno Domini Publishing
1 Churchgates, The Wilderness, Berkhamsted, Herts HP4 2UB England
Text copyright © 2007 AD Publishing, Leena Lane
Illustrations copyright © 2007 Chris Saunderson

Editorial Director Annette Reynolds
Editor Nicola Bull
Art Director Gerald Rogers
Pre-production Krystyna Kowalska Hewitt
Production John Laister

All rights reserved

Printed and bound in China